So Everything is Broken

By: Dr. Joe Mucha

I.   Introduction

In recent years, it has become increasingly clear that the social, political, and security fabric of our society is under strain. From rising poverty and income inequality to political polarization and division, to growing concerns about crime and public safety, it seems like everything is broken.

In this book, we aim to delve into the root causes of these challenges and explore their impact on individuals, communities, and society. We will examine the ways in which government institutions, private businesses, non-profit organizations, and communities are grappling with these issues, and consider the role that individuals can play in helping to address them. While the challenges we face are daunting, they are not insurmountable. By coming together and working collaboratively, we can help to create a more just, equitable, and secure future for all. Whether you are a concerned citizen, an advocate for social change, or simply looking for ways to make a difference in your community, this book is for you. Join us on a journey of discovery, as we seek to understand and address the social, political, and security challenges of our time.

A. The state of social, political and security issues in the United States

The United States is facing a complex array of social, political, and security issues that threaten to undermine the foundations of American society. These challenges are deeply interconnected, and their impacts are far-reaching and far-reaching, affecting individuals, families, communities, and the nation.

At the social level, the United States is grappling with rising poverty and income inequality, a lack of support systems for vulnerable populations, and growing concerns about the well-being of its citizens. Despite being one of the wealthiest nations in the world, millions of Americans live in poverty, unable to meet their basic needs or access the resources they need to thrive. This is particularly true for communities of color, who are disproportionately affected by poverty and lack of access to resources. The lack of support systems for vulnerable populations, such as the elderly, disabled, and homeless, exacerbates these challenges and leaves many Americans without the help they need to survive.

The political climate in the United States is also increasingly polarized and divided, with deep disagreements over key issues and a lack of common ground. The role of money in politics is a major contributor to this division, with wealthy individuals and corporations wielding disproportionate influence over the political process. The erosion of democratic institutions and values also threatens to undermine the stability and security of the nation, as it becomes increasingly difficult for the government to address the pressing needs and concerns of the people.

In terms of security, the United States is facing growing concerns about crime and violence, both domestically and internationally. The threat of terrorism and the proliferation of weapons of mass destruction are among the greatest security challenges facing the country, and the impact of mass incarceration has had far-reaching and detrimental effects on communities and families. At the same time, many Americans are concerned about the growing threat of cybercrime and the potential for cyberattacks to disrupt critical infrastructure and compromise sensitive data.

In the face of these challenges, it is more important than ever for the United States to come together to find solutions and address the root causes of these problems. This will require collaboration between government, the private sector, and communities, as well as a renewed commitment to the principles of justice, equality, and security that have always been at the heart of American society. Only by working together can we build a more just, equitable, and secure future for all Americans.

II.   Social Challenges

A. Rising poverty and income inequality

Poverty and income inequality are two of the most pressing social challenges facing the United States today. Despite being one of the wealthiest nations in the world, millions of Americans live in poverty, struggling to meet their basic needs and access the resources they need to thrive. This not only undermines the well-being of these individuals and families, but it also has far-reaching and detrimental effects on communities and society.
Poverty is a complex and multifaceted issue that affects individuals and families in a variety of ways. People living in poverty often struggle to access quality healthcare, education, and housing, which can have a long-term impact on their health, well-being, and future opportunities. This is particularly true for children growing up in poverty, who are more likely to experience poor health outcomes, lower educational attainment, and limited economic opportunities later in life.

At the same time, income inequality has grown dramatically in recent decades, with the gap between the rich and poor widening and a shrinking middle class. This has led to an increasingly unequal distribution of wealth and resources, with the wealthiest Americans enjoying a disproportionate share of the nation's prosperity. This has contributed to a growing sense of economic insecurity and political polarization, as many Americans feel that the system is stacked against them and that their government is not working for their interests.

The root causes of poverty and income inequality are complex and interrelated and include factors such as a lack of access to quality education and training, declining wages for low- and middle-income workers, and a tax system that benefits the wealthy. Addressing these root causes will require a multi-faceted approach, including policies that promote greater access to education and training, raise the minimum wage, and reform the tax code to ensure that everyone pays their fair share.

Ultimately, reducing poverty and addressing income inequality are essential to building a more just and equitable society. This will require a renewed commitment to the principles of economic justice and equality, as well as a recognition that the well-being of every individual and community is interconnected and interdependent. Only by working together can we build a future in which every American can thrive and succeed.

B. Inadequate support systems and income inequality

The United States is facing several social challenges when it comes to supporting vulnerable populations, including those who are homeless, struggling with addiction, or living with mental illness. Despite being one of the wealthiest nations in the world, many Americans are still struggling to access the resources and support they need to meet their basic needs and lead healthy, productive lives.

Homelessness is a particularly pressing issue in many communities, with millions of people sleeping on the streets or in shelters each night. This not only undermines the well-being of these individuals, but it also has far-reaching and detrimental effects on communities and society as a whole. People who are homeless are more likely to experience poor health outcomes, lower educational attainment, and limited economic opportunities, and are more likely to be involved in the criminal justice system.

Similarly, individuals struggling with addiction and mental illness often face significant barriers to accessing quality healthcare and support. Despite being treatable conditions, many people do not receive the care and treatment they need, either due to lack of insurance coverage or stigma associated with these conditions. This can lead to a cycle of poverty, incarceration, and poor health outcomes that can be difficult to break.

Another key challenge is the lack of adequate support systems for elderly and disabled populations, who may struggle to access quality healthcare, housing, and transportation. This can limit their ability to remain independent and engaged in their communities and can also place a significant burden on their families and caregivers.

Ultimately, addressing these social challenges will require a multi-faceted approach, including policies that promote greater access to quality healthcare and support, investment in affordable housing and transportation, and targeted resources for the most vulnerable populations. This will require a renewed commitment to the principles of compassion and dignity, and a recognition that the well-being of every individual and community is interconnected and interdependent. Only by working together can we build a future in which every American has the opportunity to thrive and succeed.

C. The impact of these challenges on individuals and communities

The social challenges facing vulnerable populations in the United States today have a profound and far-reaching impact on both individuals and communities. These challenges, which include poverty, homelessness, addiction, mental illness, and inadequate support systems for the elderly and disabled, can leave individuals feeling isolated, hopeless, and unable to meet their basic needs. At the same time, communities suffer because of increased crime, lower property values, and reduced economic opportunities.
One of the most significant impacts of these social challenges is poverty. When individuals and families are unable to make ends meet, they may struggle to access quality healthcare, safe and affordable housing, and nutritious food. This can lead to a cycle of poverty that is difficult to break and can have lasting effects on individuals and their children, including lower educational attainment and reduced economic opportunities.
Homelessness is another pressing challenge that has a profound impact on individuals and communities. People who are homeless are more likely to experience poor health outcomes, and are at increased risk of exposure to crime, violence, and victimization. This not only undermines the well-being of these individuals, but it also has far-reaching effects on communities and society, reducing property values, limiting economic opportunities, and increasing the burden on emergency services and hospitals.
Similarly, individuals struggling with addiction and mental illness often face significant barriers to accessing quality healthcare and support, including a lack of insurance coverage, stigma, and discrimination. This can lead to a cycle of poverty, incarceration, and poor health outcomes that can be difficult to break and can have lasting effects on individuals and their families.
Another key challenge is the lack of adequate support systems for elderly and disabled populations, who may struggle to access quality healthcare, housing, and transportation. This can limit their ability to remain independent and engaged in their communities and can also place a significant burden on their families and caregivers.
The impact of these social challenges extends beyond individual and families and affects entire communities. When vulnerable populations are

unable to access quality healthcare, safe and affordable housing, and support, this can increase crime, reduce property values, and limit economic opportunities.

The social challenges facing vulnerable populations in the United States today have a profound and far-reaching impact on both individuals and communities. Addressing these challenges will require a multi-faceted approach, including policies that promote greater access to quality healthcare and support, investment in affordable housing and transportation, and targeted resources for the most vulnerable populations.

III.   Political Challenges

A. Political polarization and division

The political landscape of the United States has seen a rise in polarization and division in recent years, with citizens increasingly separating into two distinct camps with vastly different opinions and values. This political divide has led to a breakdown in the democratic process, with politicians from both parties becoming entrenched in their positions and unwilling to compromise. This lack of cooperation has made it difficult, if not impossible, for the government to effectively address the pressing issues facing the country, leading to frustration and disillusionment among the general public.

One of the key challenges of political polarization and division is the inability of the government to pass meaningful legislation. Political polarization has led to a lack of cooperation between the two major political parties, making it difficult for bills to pass through both houses of Congress. This has left important issues, such as healthcare reform, immigration, and gun control, unresolved, leading to a growing sense of frustration and anger among citizens.

Another challenge of political polarization and division is the rise of extremism. As people become more entrenched in their political beliefs, they are increasingly likely to embrace extreme positions and ideologies. This has led to an increase in hate crimes, political violence, and domestic terrorism, creating a dangerous and unstable political environment.

The impact of political polarization and division is felt far beyond the halls of Congress and the White House. It affects individuals and communities across the country, eroding trust in government and breaking down social cohesion. When citizens are divided and unable to come together to address common problems, it creates a sense of hopelessness and cynicism, making it difficult for them to believe that the political system can ever work for their benefit.

The political challenges of polarization and division in the USA today are significant and far-reaching, affecting individuals, communities, and the country as a whole. To overcome these challenges, it is imperative that citizens come together to demand that their elected officials work towards bridging the political divide and finding common solutions to the problems facing the nation.

B. The role of money in politics

The role of money in politics has long been a contentious issue in the United States, and it remains a major challenge for the country today. The influence of money in politics undermines the democratic process by giving wealthy individuals and corporations an outsized voice in the political system, at the expense of ordinary citizens.

One of the key challenges of the role of money in politics is the corrupting influence it can have on elected officials. When politicians rely on large campaign donations from wealthy donors to fund their campaigns, they are more likely to be influenced by the interests of those donors rather than the interests of their constituents. This creates a situation in which elected officials are beholden to their donors, rather than the citizens they were elected to represent, leading to policies that favor the wealthy at the expense of everyone else.

Another challenge of the role of money in politics is the unequal representation it creates. Wealthy individuals and corporations have the resources to make large campaign donations, while ordinary citizens do not. This creates a situation in which the political system is dominated by the interests of the wealthy, leaving the needs and concerns of the average citizen unrepresented.

The impact of the role of money in politics is felt by individuals and communities across the country. When elected officials are more responsive to the needs of their wealthy donors than to the needs of their constituents, it creates a sense of disconnection and disillusionment among citizens. This can lead to a breakdown in trust in government and a general sense of frustration and anger.

The political challenge of the role of money in politics in the USA is a serious one that has far-reaching impacts on the country and its citizens. To overcome this challenge, it is essential that citizens demand that their elected officials take steps to reduce the influence of money in politics and ensure that the political system works for everyone, not just the wealthy few. By taking action and speaking out against the corrupting influence of money in politics, we can help to create a more democratic and representative political system that serves the interests of all citizens.

C. The erosion of democratic institutions and values

The erosion of democratic institutions and values in the United States is a growing political challenge that threatens the very foundation of American democracy. In recent years, there has been a disturbing trend of politicians and political leaders disregarding fundamental democratic norms and institutions, leading to a decline in public trust in government and a sense of disillusionment among citizens.

One of the key challenges of the erosion of democratic institutions and values is the attack on the independence of the judiciary. In many cases, politicians have attempted to interfere with the functioning of the courts, undermining the principle of the separation of powers and eroding the rule of law. This creates a situation in which the judiciary is no longer able to provide an independent check on the actions of the executive and legislative branches, leaving citizens without a means of holding their government accountable.

Another challenge is the suppression of free speech and the press. When political leaders seek to control the narrative and silence dissenting voices, it undermines the free exchange of ideas and information that is essential to a functioning democracy. This creates a situation in which citizens are not able to access the information they need to make informed decisions, leading to a breakdown in trust in government and a general sense of disillusionment.

The erosion of democratic institutions and values also affects the functioning of the political system itself. When politicians disregard democratic norms, it creates a culture of corruption and undermines the legitimacy of government. This can lead to a breakdown in the rule of law, a loss of faith in the political system, and a sense of disunity and division among citizens.

The political challenge of the erosion of democratic institutions and values in the United States is a serious one that requires the attention and action of all citizens. To overcome this challenge, it is essential that we stand up for democratic norms and institutions, and demand that our elected officials respect the rule of law and protect the independence of the judiciary, the freedom of speech and the press, and other essential democratic values.

IV.   Security Challenges

A. The threat of crime and violence

The issue of crime and violence in the United States has long been a concern for individuals and communities alike. While crime rates have fluctuated over the years, the recent surge in violence in certain parts of the country has caused alarm for many Americans. The problem is multi-faceted and encompasses various factors including poverty, drug addiction, gang activity, and inadequate funding for law enforcement and social programs.

One of the most pressing challenges posed by crime and violence is the negative impact it has on individuals and communities. For those directly affected by crime, the emotional, psychological, and financial toll can be devastating. For communities, crime can lead to a decline in property values, increased stress and anxiety, and a general sense of insecurity.

Another major challenge posed by crime and violence is the strain it places on law enforcement and the criminal justice system. In many areas, law enforcement is understaffed and underfunded, making it difficult to effectively respond to and investigate crimes. Additionally, the criminal justice system is often criticized for being overly punitive and not addressing the root causes of crime.

Furthermore, the issue of crime and violence is often exacerbated by structural inequalities, particularly those related to race and socioeconomic status. Communities of color are disproportionately affected by crime, and individuals living in poverty are more likely to be both victims and perpetrators of crime.

To address the challenges posed by crime and violence, a multi-pronged approach is necessary. This should include increased funding for law enforcement and social programs, as well as a focus on addressing the root causes of crime, such as poverty and drug addiction. Additionally, efforts should be made to address structural inequalities and ensure that the criminal justice system is more equitable and effective.

The issue of crime and violence in the United States is a complex and pressing one that demands the attention of individuals, communities, and the government alike.

B. The impact of mass incarceration

The issue of mass incarceration in the United States has become a major security challenge in recent years. Mass incarceration refers to the high rate of imprisonment in the country, where more than 2 million people are currently incarcerated. This has far-reaching implications for individuals, families, and communities, as well as for the broader social, economic, and political landscape of the country.

One of the key drivers of mass incarceration in the United States is the War on Drugs, which was declared in the 1980s and 1990s. This policy aimed to reduce drug use and drug trafficking by increasing arrests, mandatory minimum sentences, and other forms of punishment. However, this approach has been criticized for being too heavy-handed, as it has resulted in large numbers of people being sentenced to long prison terms for minor drug offenses.

Another factor contributing to mass incarceration is the trend of "tough on crime" policies, which have been implemented in response to public concerns about crime and safety. These policies have led to the creation of mandatory sentences, "three strikes" laws, and other measures that increase the likelihood of people being incarcerated for longer periods of time.

The impact of mass incarceration on individuals and communities has been significant. For those who are incarcerated, their lives are often dramatically altered, as they face physical and emotional hardship, as well as a loss of freedom and autonomy. Their families are also affected, as they are often left without a primary source of financial support and may struggle to maintain relationships with their loved ones.

In addition to the direct impact on individuals and families, mass incarceration has broader implications for communities, particularly communities of color, which are disproportionately impacted by the criminal justice system. For example, mass incarceration has contributed to poverty and unemployment, as those who are incarcerated face significant barriers to finding work upon their release.

Furthermore, mass incarceration has a significant impact on the economy, as billions of dollars are spent on the criminal justice system each year. This money could be better spent on programs and services that support vulnerable populations and help to reduce crime and violence.

The issue of mass incarceration in the United States is a complex and challenging one, with far-reaching implications for individuals, families, and communities. It is important to continue to critically examine this issue and explore solutions that can help to reduce the number of people who are incarcerated, while also ensuring public safety and protecting the rights and freedoms of all individuals.

C. The challenges of ensuring public safety in an uncertain world

The United States is facing numerous security challenges in an increasingly uncertain world. The threat of crime and violence, mass incarceration, and the need to ensure public safety are among the most pressing of these challenges. While the country has always been a beacon of hope and stability, the rapidly changing world and the challenges it brings have made it increasingly difficult to maintain that position.

One of the major security challenges in the USA today is the increasing levels of crime and violence. Despite numerous efforts to reduce crime rates and make communities safer, many cities and communities continue to be plagued by high levels of violent crime. This has a devastating impact on the individuals and families who are directly affected, as well as on the broader community. The fear of crime and the impact it has on people's lives can erode social cohesion, undermine trust in law enforcement, and create an environment in which people are more likely to take the law into their own hands.

Another major security challenge in the USA is mass incarceration. The country has one of the highest incarceration rates in the world, and this has had a significant impact on communities, particularly communities of color. The over-reliance on imprisonment as a form of punishment has not only failed to reduce crime, but it has also created a host of social and economic problems for those who are incarcerated and their families. The high cost of mass incarceration has put a strain on government budgets, while the social and economic costs have had a negative impact on communities, particularly those that are already struggling.

Finally, the USA is facing the challenge of ensuring public safety in an uncertain world. The threat of terrorism, cyberattacks, and other forms of violence have made it increasingly difficult to guarantee the safety of citizens. At the same time, the changing nature of work and the increased vulnerability of individuals and communities to natural disasters and other forms of crisis have made it more important than ever to have strong security systems in place.

The USA is facing numerous security challenges, each of which is having a profound impact on individuals, communities, and the country as a whole. It is imperative that the country takes these challenges seriously and works to find solutions that will ensure public safety and promote social stability. Only by working together to address these challenges can the country hope to maintain its position as a leader and a beacon of hope in an uncertain world.

V.   Education and the Future

A. The state of the education system

The state of the education system in the United States is a subject of much debate and concern. Despite being one of the wealthiest nations in the world, the American education system is facing a range of challenges that are negatively impacting students and their future prospects. These challenges include inadequate funding, declining enrollment, teacher shortages, and a persistent achievement gap between students of different races and socio-economic backgrounds.

One of the most significant challenges facing the education system in the United States is inadequate funding. Many schools, particularly in low-income areas, are struggling to provide students with the resources they need to succeed. This can mean overcrowded classrooms, outdated textbooks and technology, and limited opportunities for extracurricular activities. The lack of funding also affects the ability of schools to attract and retain high-quality teachers, which can have a negative impact on student achievement.

Another challenge is declining enrollment, which is a result of factors such as declining birth rates, immigration policies, and shifting demographics. This has the potential to reduce the pool of talent available to future generations and could limit the economic growth and competitiveness of the country.

Teacher shortages are another challenge facing the education system in the United States. The shortage of teachers, particularly in subjects such as mathematics, science, and special education, is making it difficult for schools to provide students with a quality education. This shortage is also contributing to the achievement gap between students of different races and socio-economic backgrounds, as students in low-income areas are more likely to be taught by inexperienced or uncertified teachers.

Finally, the persistent achievement gap between students of different races and socio-economic backgrounds is one of the most pressing challenges facing the education system in the United States. This gap is largely a result of factors such as poverty, inadequate funding, and unequal access to quality education. Despite efforts to close the achievement gap, it remains a persistent problem and one that is having a negative impact on the future prospects of millions of American students.

The state of the education system in the United States is of great concern, as it has the potential to impact the future prospects of students and the competitiveness of the country. It is essential that policymakers and educators take action to address these challenges and ensure that all students have access to a quality education. This includes increasing funding for education, attracting and retaining high-quality teachers, and addressing the persistent achievement gap between students of different races and socio-economic backgrounds.

B. The importance of investing in education for a secure and equitable future

The state of education in the United States has been a topic of concern for many years, with debates surrounding funding, standardized testing, and the role of schools in society. Despite these challenges, it is clear that investing in education is critical for a secure and equitable future.

Education plays a key role in providing individuals with the skills and knowledge needed to succeed in today's rapidly changing job market. As technology continues to transform the economy, workers will need to be equipped with new and adaptable skills in order to remain competitive. Investing in education is the best way to ensure that workers are equipped with the skills they need to succeed.

Additionally, education is critical for promoting social mobility and reducing income inequality. Studies have shown that individuals with higher levels of education are more likely to have higher-paying jobs and greater earning potential. Furthermore, a well-funded and high-quality education system can provide children from disadvantaged backgrounds with the tools and resources they need to overcome their circumstances and reach their full potential.

Investing in education also has long-term benefits for society as a whole. A well-educated population leads to a more informed and engaged citizenry, which is essential for a thriving democracy. In addition, education can play a role in reducing crime, promoting social cohesion, and building more resilient communities.

Despite the clear benefits of investing in education, many states and communities are facing budget constraints and political pressure to cut funding for schools. This is a short-sighted approach that ignores the long-term benefits of a well-educated population. Rather than cutting funding for education, policymakers should be working to find creative and sustainable solutions that will ensure that every student has access to a high-quality education.

Investing in education is critical for securing a prosperous and equitable future. By equipping individuals with the skills and knowledge they need to succeed, promoting social mobility, and building stronger and more resilient communities, education has the power to shape the future and address some of the most pressing social and political challenges of our time.

C. The role of individuals in supporting education and lifelong learning

Education is the foundation for the future of individuals and society. It provides individuals with the skills, knowledge, and critical thinking abilities necessary to succeed in a rapidly changing world. With advancements in technology, automation, and artificial intelligence, it is increasingly important for individuals to be lifelong learners and continue to adapt and evolve their skillset. In the United States, the education system is facing numerous challenges, including underfunding, unequal opportunities, and a lack of support for lifelong learning. Despite these challenges, investing in education remains crucial for a secure and equitable future.

The role of individuals in supporting education and lifelong learning is essential. This includes supporting funding for public education, advocating for policies that prioritize education and access to opportunities for lifelong learning. Furthermore, individuals can take an active role in their own education by seeking out opportunities for learning and development, and encouraging others to do the same. By investing in their own education, individuals can better equip themselves to succeed in the future and help to create a more equitable society.

In today's world, the pace of change is rapid, and individuals need to be prepared to continuously adapt and evolve. Investing in education and lifelong learning is a way for individuals to take control of their future, build resilience and prepare for a rapidly changing world. By prioritizing education and lifelong learning, individuals can help create a more equitable and secure future for themselves and future generations.

VI.   Finding Solutions

A. The role of government in addressing social, political and security
   challenges

The United States is facing a number of complex social, political, and
security challenges that threaten the stability and prosperity of its citizens and
communities. In order to address these challenges and move towards a more
equitable and secure future, it is important to consider the role of government
in finding solutions.

One of the key social challenges facing the United States today is
poverty and income inequality. Despite being one of the wealthiest countries
in the world, millions of Americans live in poverty and struggle to make ends
meet. Government has a role to play in addressing this issue through policies
that increase access to education and job training, provide a safety net for
those in need, and raise the minimum wage to ensure that work provides a
path out of poverty.

Another major challenge is the erosion of democratic institutions and
values in the United States. The increasing polarization of political discourse,
the influence of money in politics, and the decline of trust in government
institutions all threaten to undermine the foundations of American
democracy. Government has a role to play in restoring public trust and
strengthening democratic institutions, through reforms that increase
transparency and accountability, limit the influence of money in politics, and
promote bipartisanship and cooperation in the political process.

When it comes to security, the United States is facing a number of
serious challenges, including crime and violence, the impact of mass
incarceration, and the challenges of ensuring public safety in an uncertain
world. Government has a role to play in addressing these challenges by
investing in programs and initiatives that prevent crime and reduce
recidivism, reform the criminal justice system to reduce mass incarceration,
and enhance public safety through improved policing, community-oriented
strategies, and investments in crime prevention and early intervention.

Education is another critical area where government has a key role to
play in shaping the future of the United States. By investing in education and
promoting lifelong learning, government can help ensure that all Americans
have the skills and knowledge they need to succeed in the 21st century. This

could include initiatives that increase access to early childhood education, improve K-12 schools, and provide affordable college and job training opportunities.

Ultimately, the challenges facing the United States today require collective action and cooperation at all levels of government and society. By working together and taking a proactive approach to addressing these issues, we can create a more equitable, secure, and prosperous future for all Americans.

B. The importance of community engagement and activism

In the United States today, there are numerous social, political, and security challenges that threaten the stability and well-being of individuals and communities. These challenges include poverty, income inequality, inadequate support systems for vulnerable populations, political polarization and division, the erosion of democratic institutions and values, crime and violence, mass incarceration, and an underperforming education system, among others. Despite the severity and complexity of these problems, there is hope that they can be addressed through community engagement and activism.

Community engagement and activism refer to the active participation of citizens in shaping the policies and practices that affect their lives. It involves the use of collective action and advocacy to raise awareness about issues, influence decision-makers, and promote social change. Community engagement and activism have been instrumental in bringing about significant reforms in the past and have the potential to bring about meaningful change in the present and future.

One of the key benefits of community engagement and activism is that it helps to ensure that the voices of marginalized communities are heard. When individuals and communities participate in advocacy and activism, they are able to bring attention to issues that are often ignored or neglected by those in positions of power. This can lead to policies and practices that are more responsive to the needs of marginalized communities and can help to reduce poverty, improve access to resources and services, and promote social justice.

Another benefit of community engagement and activism is that it can bring about systemic change. Through collective action and advocacy, citizens can push for reforms in policies, institutions, and systems that perpetuate social and political challenges. For example, community activism can help to reduce mass incarceration by advocating for criminal justice reforms that promote rehabilitation and alternatives to imprisonment. Similarly, community engagement and activism can help to improve the quality of education by advocating for increased investment in schools, teachers, and students.

Community engagement and activism play a critical role in finding solutions to the social, political, and security challenges facing the United States today. By empowering individuals and communities to participate in shaping the policies and practices that affect their lives, community engagement and activism can help to ensure that marginalized communities are heard, bring about systemic change, and create a more equitable and just society.

C. The value of individual self-reliance, self-protective and self-motivation

In the current state of the United States, there are numerous challenges affecting the lives of citizens on multiple fronts. Social, political, and security issues are prevalent, and they are putting a strain on the ability of individuals, communities, and the government to maintain a stable, prosperous, and secure society. As a result, many are looking for ways to address these problems, and one possible solution is for individuals to take a more proactive and self-reliant approach.

Self-reliance, self-protection, and self-motivation are traits that can help individuals better navigate the challenges they face in their daily lives. Self-reliance involves having the skills and resources necessary to meet one's own needs and handle problems independently. This can include having financial independence, developing practical skills, and building strong relationships with others. Self-protection involves taking steps to keep oneself and one's family safe, such as being prepared for emergencies, practicing self-defense, and seeking out trusted sources of information. Self-motivation involves setting goals and taking actions to achieve them, and it is a critical component of success in life.

While the government has an important role to play in addressing social, political, and security challenges, individuals can also make a significant impact. By becoming more self-reliant, self-protective, and self-motivated, individuals can create a more secure and stable environment for themselves and those around them. For example, individuals who are financially independent can weather economic downturns, those who have practical skills can help others in their community, and those who are self-motivated can drive positive change in their communities.

Moreover, a self-reliant, self-protective, and self-motivated population can put pressure on the government to improve its own services and policies. When individuals can take care of themselves and their communities, the government is less likely to take advantage of their dependency, and will instead be more accountable to the needs and desires of its citizens. While social, political, and security challenges in the USA are complex and widespread, individuals can play a critical role in addressing these issues. By becoming more self-reliant, self-protective, and self-motivated, individuals can create a more stable, secure, and prosperous society, and exert a positive influence on their communities and the government.

While many of these challenges can seem insurmountable, there are steps that individuals can take to mitigate their impact and strive for a better future. One such step is the adoption of individual self-reliance, self-protection, and self-motivation.

Self-reliance involves taking responsibility for one's own well-being and relying on oneself rather than others or external factors. This means making a conscious effort to cultivate the skills, knowledge, and resources necessary to thrive in today's society. It involves being proactive in seeking opportunities for growth and development, and taking steps to improve one's financial, physical, and emotional health.

Self-protection involves taking measures to protect oneself and one's loved ones from harm. This includes both physical safety and financial security. For example, individuals can take steps to protect their personal information, invest in their health and well-being, and plan for their financial future. By taking these steps, individuals can reduce their risk of becoming victims of crime or suffering from financial hardship.

Finally, self-motivation involves having the drive and determination to achieve one's goals and aspirations. This can involve setting and working towards personal and professional goals, seeking out new challenges, and continuously learning and growing. By being self-motivated, individuals can create a more fulfilling life for themselves, build stronger relationships, and make a positive impact on their communities.

Adopting a mindset of individual self-reliance, self-protection, and self-motivation is one step that individuals can take to mitigate the impact of social, political, and security challenges in the USA. By taking responsibility for their own well-being and striving for self-improvement, individuals can build a more secure and equitable future for themselves and their communities.

D. The power of collaboration and working together.

The challenges facing the United States today are complex and multifaceted, ranging from social issues such as poverty and inequality, to political issues such as division and the role of money in politics, to security issues such as crime and mass incarceration. While these challenges may seem overwhelming, there is hope for finding solutions and improving the future of the country. One such solution lies in the power of collaboration and working together.

In order to address the challenges facing the country, it is important for individuals, communities, and government to work together towards a common goal. Collaboration fosters a sense of community and unity, bringing people together to tackle complex problems and find innovative solutions. By working together, people can pool their resources, knowledge, and expertise, leading to more effective and efficient problem-solving.

In addition to collaboration, individuals also have a critical role to play in supporting education and lifelong learning, and in being self-reliant, self-protective, and self-motivated. Education provides individuals with the knowledge and skills necessary to succeed in an ever-changing world, while self-reliance and self-motivation help individuals take control of their own lives and make positive changes.

At the same time, government also has a critical role to play in addressing the challenges facing the country. This can include investing in education and supporting programs that help vulnerable populations, as well as working to reform the criminal justice system and address issues of crime and mass incarceration.

Finding solutions to the challenges facing the United States will require a combination of individual effort, community engagement and activism, and government action. By working together, people can create a future that is more equitable, secure, and prosperous for all.

The challenges of poverty and income inequality, inadequate support systems for vulnerable populations, political polarization and division, the erosion of democratic institutions and values, crime and violence, mass incarceration, and the state of education are among the most pressing issues that must be addressed. In order to find effective solutions, it is important to consider the role of various actors, including the government, communities, and individuals.

One key solution is the importance of community engagement and activism. Through active involvement in local and national discussions and decision-making processes, individuals can help to shape the policies and programs that affect their lives and communities. This can involve participating in elections, advocacy efforts, community organizing, and other forms of activism. By working together, communities can hold elected officials accountable, support policies that promote social and economic justice, and help to address the root causes of social and political challenges.

Another solution is the value of individual self-reliance, self-protection, and self-motivation. While government and community efforts are critical to creating a more equitable and just society, individuals also have a role to play in creating positive change. By taking control of their own lives, individuals can empower themselves and their communities. This can involve making responsible financial decisions, pursuing education and training, developing skills and abilities, and engaging in healthy and safe behaviors.

The power of collaboration and working together must not be underestimated. While individual efforts are important, collective action can achieve far more than any one person can alone. By coming together across communities, organizations, and movements, individuals can pool their resources and expertise, amplify their voices, and effect real change. Collaboration and partnerships can help to break down the silos that often divide people and communities and foster a sense of shared responsibility and common purpose.

There are many social, political, and security challenges facing the United States today, but there are also many opportunities for positive change. By working together, by empowering individuals and communities, and by pursuing a common vision of a more equitable and just society, it is possible to create a brighter future for all.

VII.   Conclusion

A. Reflections on the journey of the book

The United States is facing numerous social, political, and security challenges that have a profound impact on individuals and communities. Issues such as poverty and income inequality, inadequate support systems for vulnerable populations, political polarization and division, the role of money in politics, the erosion of democratic institutions and values, crime and violence, mass incarceration, public safety in an uncertain world, the state of the education system, and the importance of lifelong learning, all play a role in shaping the future of our country.

While these challenges are complex and multifaceted, they can be addressed through a combination of government action, community engagement and activism, individual self-reliance and self-motivation, and collaboration and working together. The power of collective action cannot be underestimated, as it has the potential to bring about meaningful change and progress in addressing the social, political, and security challenges facing the United States.

It is important to recognize that the future of the United States is not determined by any one individual or group, but rather by the collective actions of all its citizens. It is up to us to work together to find solutions and build a better future for ourselves and for generations to come. Whether through government action, community engagement, individual self-reliance, or collaboration and teamwork, we must each play our part in ensuring a secure and equitable future for all.

B. The importance of continued action and advocacy

The importance of continued action and advocacy should not be overlooked if solutions are to be found and implemented. Here is a list of some actions that each group can take to help fix these issues:

Individuals:
1.   Educate themselves on the issues: Individuals can educate themselves on the social, political, security, and education challenges facing

the country by reading books, watching documentaries, and participating in discussions and debates.

2.	Vote: Individuals can use their right to vote to elect leaders who share their values and who are committed to addressing the country's most pressing problems.

3.	Advocate for change: Individuals can advocate for change by writing letters to their elected officials, participating in protests and demonstrations, and by joining advocacy organizations.

4.	Donate to organizations: Individuals can donate money to organizations working to address the social, political, security, and education challenges facing the country.

Communities:

1.	Build coalitions: Communities can build coalitions with other organizations and groups to leverage their collective power and influence.

2.	Advocate for change: Communities can advocate for change by organizing town hall meetings, participating in demonstrations, and by writing letters to their elected officials.

3.	Provide resources: Communities can provide resources, such as food, clothing, and shelter, to those who are struggling.

4.	Create education programs: Communities can create education programs to help their residents access the education they need to succeed.

Government:

1.	Implement policies: The government can implement policies to address the social, political, security, and education challenges facing the country.

2.	Invest in education: The government can invest in education by providing funding for schools, colleges, and universities.

3.	Improve access to healthcare: The government can improve access to healthcare by expanding Medicaid and by creating policies that make healthcare more affordable for all Americans.

4.	Strengthen national security: The government can strengthen national security by investing in the military, by strengthening cybersecurity, and by working with other countries to address global security threats.

These are just some of the actions that individuals, communities, and the government can take to address the social, political, security, and education challenges facing America. The important thing is to take action, and to continue advocating for change, even when progress seems slow or elusive. So everything is broken, but together we decide if it stays broken.